How the world makes music

Iwo and Pamela Zaluski

Young Library

Contents

How do woodwind instruments work?

The basic sound of woodwind instruments is made by such devices as blowing across the top of a bottle, blowing across a blade of grass held tightly between the thumbs, blowing through the pages of an exercise book, or even just by whistling. These initial squeaks are then controlled by the player to produce musical notes.

The instruments are played by blowing into a tube through a mouthpiece, which is the part that produces the squeak. Most woodwind mouthpieces use some form of reed. This is a thin 'wafer' of wood, or sometimes brass, which acts like a blade of grass to produce the squeak.

When the player has 'squeaked' into the mouthpiece, the air carrying the squeak vibrates as it passes down the tube and out of the holes in the side. The pitch of the note depends on how far the air must travel before it can escape: the further the distance, the lower the sound.

Orchestral woodwind instruments use padded keys to cover the holes. These must be certain distances apart, and it is sometimes difficult for the fingers to stretch far enough. So the keys act as remote controls to cover or uncover holes out of reach. Players must learn to master these keys, just as a recorder player learns to master the eight holes of the recorder.

pads over holes   keys

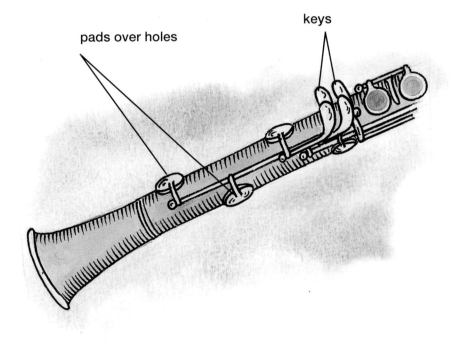

The tube acts as a sound-box, and turns the original squeak into a musical sound. Most tubes are made of wood, metal, or plastic.

Some woodwind instruments, such as the harmonium and the accordion, are pumped instead of blown.

Accordion

Accordions are nicknamed 'squeezeboxes', because the player pumps air into two panels of reeds, each held in one hand. The panels are joined by a bellows, which is worked by pumping with the hands.

One panel is like a piano keyboard, for playing tunes. The other uses buttons, which play accompaniment chords.

The reeds are made of tiny rectangular metal frames. A thin metal strip attached to one end almost, but not quite, covers the hole in the metal frame. The other end is loose, and vibrates when air is pumped through it. The bigger the reed, the lower the note.

The accordion is featured in the folk music of many lands.

Smaller accordions

Small, hand-held mouth organs, or **harmonicas**, also use metal reeds, but are blown, not pumped. **Concertinas** and **bandoleons** are like accordions, but are smaller and have buttons only.

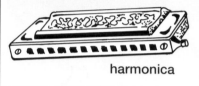

harmonica

Folk dancing

Accordions have a loud, tinny sound, and are used in folk dancing and Argentine tangos.

Some great harmonica players

Larry Adler
Tommy Reilly

Bagpipes

Bagpipes look like a windbag with pipes sticking out of it. They are played by first blowing air into the bag through the windpipe. The player then pumps the bag, pushing the air through the 'chanter'. The chanter is a pipe containing a double reed and finger holes. The reed acts like two blades of grass, making a wheezy sound. The chanter is played by covering and uncovering the finger holes.

Most bagpipes have two extra chanters, which have no finger holes. They are each tuned to play one note only, and serve as a monotonous, unchanging accompaniment called a 'drone'.

The bag is kept filled with air. The player does not stop playing to take a breath. He just makes sure air is always passing through the chanter, so bagpipe music is continuous.

The Scottish bagpipes provide exciting music to march to, and are used in many ceremonial occasions.

Martial music

Bagpipes are used in folk music throughout the world, especially Scotland and Ireland, and in military parades.

Bassoon

The bassoon is sometimes known as the joker of the orchestra because of its low, reedy sound.

The bassoon plays the bass notes of the woodwind section in an orchestra. It is made of wood, and uses a double wooden reed to make its first sound. It has an arrangement of holes and keys which are played with the fingers.

As it is the longest woodwind instrument, it plays the lowest notes. The wooden tube is two-and-a-half metres long and has to be 'folded' in half, so that the player can reach the keys and holes. The mouthpiece is on the end of a curved metal tube. This is also folded over so that it can reach the player's mouth.

The musical clown

Tunes do not sound good on a bassoon, except for funny effects. This is why it is sometimes called the clown of the orchestra.

Lower than low

The **contra-bassoon** is even longer, for extra low notes. It plays an octave lower than the bassoon.

Clarinet

The clarinet was invented 300 years ago in Germany. It uses a single wooden reed which almost covers an opening in the mouthpiece. The air blown through this gap makes an ear-splitting screech, which the player turns into music by squeezing the reed with the lower lip, and by fingering the keys.

It has the biggest range of the orchestral woodwinds, and is the most expressive. Its highest notes are piercing, and its low notes are rich and mellow. Mozart wrote some of the most beautiful tunes for it.

Clarinets can bray, cry, and 'bend' notes. They can produce low, whispering tones, which make them popular with jazz musicians, who can almost make them 'talk'.

Clarinets are great favourites among jazz and swing musicians.

Family members

Similar to the clarinet is the lower-range **basset horn**. The longer **bass clarinet** is bent upwards at the bell, and is curved at the neck, so that the player can reach the keys.

bass clarinet

Some great players

Classical:
Jack Brymer
Emma Johnstone

Jazz:
Benny Goodman
Artie Shaw

Flute

Flutes date back to ancient Egypt. They are made of metal or wood. Nowadays they are held sideways. The player blows across an opening on the side of the mouth-piece, as if blowing across the top of a bottle. The angle must be just right to make a sound.

The flute plays the high notes of an orchestra's woodwind section. Like the recorder, the flute uses no reed. The two instruments make similar sounds, and until 200 years ago recorders were used in orchestras instead of flutes. Because of its clear, bright tone, the flute is often used as a solo instrument, and tunes sound very good on it.

Smaller flutes

The **piccolo** is the smallest of the flute family, and plays an octave higher. The **fife** is similar to the piccolo, and is used in military bands.

This flute is made of metal but they can also be made of wood.

Some great flautists

James Galway
Jean-Pierre Rampal

Oboe

The double reed of the oboe produces a distinctive nasal sound.

Cor anglais

The **cor anglais** (pronounced core onglay) is similar to the oboe. It is longer, slightly curved, and has a bulge at the bell. Its range is lower, and its haunting tone is very effective for sad melodies.

The oboe was first used in the Middle Ages in France, where it was called the haut-bois (pronounced or-bwah) which means 'high wood'. It is made of wood and has a double reed in the mouth-piece. This makes a squeaky noise, like blowing through two blades of grass. It is played with fingers on keys and holes.

The oboe makes a piercing, nasal sound, and is very effective when playing tunes. Like the flute, the oboe plays the high notes of a woodwind section of an orchestra, but the different tone gives variety to the sound. There are usually two oboes in an orchestra.

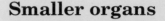

Organ

The church organ has up to four manuals, or keyboards; a windchest; and giant metal pipes each tuned to play one note. The longer the pipe, the lower the note. Because organs are so enormous, some have to be built into the church.

Air is pumped into the pipes. Each key activates its own pipe. The pump, once worked by an assistant, is today driven by electricity.

Organs have pull-out control knobs called stops, each with its own sound. With four manuals, a keyboard for the feet, stops, and a knee-operated volume control called a swell, the player can use many different sounds.

Smaller organs

The **harmonium** is a small organ with metal reeds and a foot pump. The portable **Indian harmonium** is played with one hand, while the other pumps the air in.

Vibrations

An organ played loudly can make a church vibrate.

An organist uses both hands and both feet. Sometimes the swells are positioned to be played by the knees.

Some great players

Classical:
Carlo Curly
Geraint Jones
Albert Schweitzer

Rock:
Keith Emerson

12

Recorder

Recorders are made of wood or plastic. The mouth-piece has two holes, the first to blow through, the second angled to make the air vibrate. It has seven finger holes and a thumb hole.

There are five members of the recorder family. The highest is the sopranino, but most beginners start with the descant. The alto, treble, and tenor are more difficult as the holes are further apart. The lowest is the bass, which also uses keys, as the lowest hole is too far away for the little finger to reach.

Most woodwind players begin by learning on a recorder, as it is cheap and popular with schools. Also the fingering is similar to orchestral woodwind instruments. A full recorder band is called a recorder consort.

Recorders were orchestral instruments until flutes took over by the eighteenth century.

Pan-pipes

Various wooden, bamboo, and reed pipes found all over the world are similar to the recorder. Pan-pipes are made of a bundle of one-note tubes, the longer the lower, tied in a row. The pipes are blown across the top.

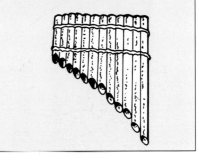

Instead of flutes

In the sixteenth and seventeenth centuries recorders were often used in orchestras as flutes.

A great Pan-pipes player

Gheorghe Zamfir

Saxophone

Saxophones were invented in Germany in 1840 by Adolphe Sax. They are made of metal, and use single reeds and keys like clarinets. There are four members in the saxophone family.

The highest and the shortest, the *soprano*, looks like a metal clarinet. The longer *alto* is curved so that the player can reach the keys. The bell is turned up. At the top of the *tenor* the tube bends upwards before bending back down again. The lowest and the longest is the *baritone*. The tube at the top 'loops the loop'. The bell is extra long.

Altos, tenors, and baritones are big and heavy. They are attached to a pendant round the player's neck, so that they hang while being played.

The noisy sax

Because of their loud, blaring tone, saxophones – especially altos and tenors – are mostly used in jazz, rock, and military bands. In orchestras they are used only for special effects.

Some great players

Soprano:
Sidney Bechet

Alto:
Charlie Parker

Tenor:
Stan Getz
Coleman Hawkins
Sonny Rollins

Baritone:
Gerry Mulligan

How *do brass instruments work?*

The basic sound of all brass instruments is made by blowing a rude noise down a tube or pipe. If the tube is wider at the end, the initial sound becomes amplified and richer. This is why all brass instruments have a wide opening, the 'bell', at the end. The sound produced is a loud strident tone.

There are two ways to alter the pitch of brass instruments. Firstly, by tightening or loosening your lips. The tighter your lips, the higher the sound.

Secondly, the longer the tube, the lower the note. Most brass instruments are made of labyrinths of tubes full of extensions and short cuts. Valves, which you press down with your fingers, either close off part of the tube, or open up another part. In this way you can make the air passage longer or shorter by the push of a button.

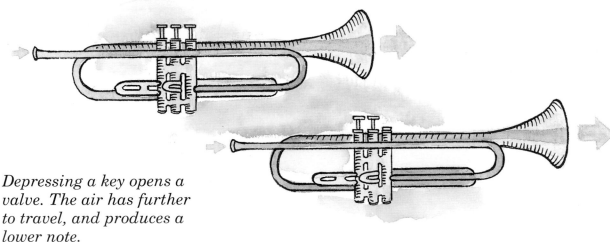

Depressing a key opens a valve. The air has further to travel, and produces a lower note.

The shape does not affect the pitch. The tubes are the same length so they have the same pitch.

Some of the earliest instruments, used by the Israelites and the Vikings, were made from the horns of cows or rams, with the pointed tips sawn off.

The alpenhorn produces a very low note indeed.

The ancient Greeks also used spiral-shaped conch shells, with the tops cut off in the same way.

To understand how brass instruments work, try blowing through tightly closed lips down any tube you can find (but make sure they are clean). Copper water pipes, or even cardboard tubes, will do. Just press hard against your lips and blow. If you do the same through a pouring funnel, you will hear the sound amplified.

French horn

The modern French horn, which has four valves, is a very long tube coiled into a circle. Its bell has a much larger diameter than most brass instruments.

It has a rich, mellow tone, a big range, and plays the medium-to-low notes in a brass section. It is often used as a solo instrument. There are up to four horns in an orchestra; but Wagner, whose music is particularly dramatic, often used eight for grand special effects.

The right hand is used to 'muffle' the sound of the horn.

Horns of the past

Horns were first made from animal horns with the point sawn off. They were also made of any handy material such as metal, shells, and hollowed-out wood. In Biblical times horn calls were used for sounding warnings. In the Middle Ages horns were used to summon people to gatherings.

Posthorns

The coiled posthorn used to announce the arrival of the mail coach. Nowadays it is often used as an ornament in restaurants and pubs. But don't be fooled, because they are usually fakes!

Some great players

Dennis Brain
Barry Tuckwell

Trombone

The first 'sackbuts', as trombones used to be called, appeared in the thirteenth century. They were used for royal fanfares and for accompanying singing in churches. Unlike trumpets at that time, they could play all the notes of the scale.

Instead of valves, trombones have a sliding tube within a tube. To alter the pitch, the player alters the length of the instrument by sliding the 'inner' tube forward or back. There are seven positions, each with its own group of notes, which are played by tightening or loosening the lips.

Nowadays, only the tenor and the lower pitched bass trombones are used, and play the medium and low notes in the brass section of an orchestra.

This boy could be accompanying on his radio a symphony orchestra or a jazz band, for the 'slide' trombone is used in both.

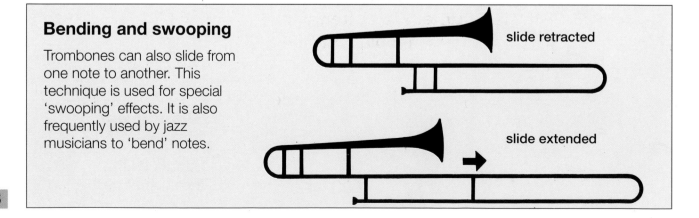

Bending and swooping

Trombones can also slide from one note to another. This technique is used for special 'swooping' effects. It is also frequently used by jazz musicians to 'bend' notes.

slide retracted

slide extended

Trumpet

Cornets are found in brass bands rather than in symphony orchestras.

The first trumpets were long, straight tubes, flared at the end. They had a smooth, detachable mouthpiece, across which the player stretched his lips. They had no valves and could only play five or six notes. According to the Bible, Joshua demolished the walls of Jericho with seven trumpets! In the fifteenth century trumpets were bent back on themselves to make them easier to hold, like the **bugle**. Soon after, valves were invented so that they could play all the notes of the scale.

Trumpets are regularly used in orchestras and brass bands, and by jazz musicians.

The high-pitched **'C'-trumpet** and the **cornet** are similar instruments, and the bugle is still used in military bands.

Ancient trumpets

Trumpets were used by the ancient Egyptians. Two were found in Tutankhamun's tomb. The Greeks used them in the Olympic Games. The Roman army used them to signal advance and retreat.

Some great players

Classical:
Hakan Hardenberger

Jazz:
Louis Armstrong
Bix Beiderbecke
Miles Davis
Dizzy Gillespie

The deep bass notes of a bombardon can sometimes make a building vibrate

Tuba

Tubas play the bass notes in the brass section of an orchestra. Its tubes are long, and shaped like a flared funnel near the bell. It is played held to the chest, with the bell pointing upwards.

Euphoniums and **tenor horns** are tubas that play the medium low notes. Smaller than tubas, they are more popular with children, who might find a tuba difficult to lift, let alone play!

The **bombardon** is the lowest tuba, and its bass notes can even make a building shake. The **sousaphone** is used in military bands as the 'oom-pah' bass. It is very long, and coiled round until it ends in a wide, curved funnel with its enormous bell pointing forward.

Tubby the Tuba

Tunes do not sound good at such a low pitch. The famous little story 'Tubby the Tuba' tells of a tuba who complains that he never has a nice tune to play.

20

How do string instruments work?

Plucking a piece of string held tightly between two solid objects makes it vibrate and produce a toneless 'ping'. This is the basic sound of a string instrument. Scraping the string instead of plucking it will produce a dull, longer sound.

The tea-chest bass of a skiffle group.

Most string instruments are made of a hollow, rounded sound box with a long neck attached. The strings are stretched from pegs at the top of the neck, over a small piece of wood called the bridge, and fixed to the bottom of the sound box. When a string is plucked or scraped, the twang (vibration) passes through the bridge into the sound box. The sound echoes, and is turned into a note. This note escapes from the sound box through cut-out holes.

The violin family are usually played with a bow – so called because it looks a bit like the bow that shoots arrows. Tightly strung horse hairs, rubbed with rosin made from the sap of trees, make the best 'scraped' sound.

The strings are made of wire, plastic, or catgut. They are tuned by tightening or loosening the pegs until they 'twang' the right note. The tighter the string, the higher the note. Different notes are produced by 'stopping' the strings with the fingers on the neck. By doing this, the player 'shortens' the string to produce a higher note.

Some string instruments, like the piano and the harpsichord, are operated by remote control using a keyboard.

The Spanish guitar is used in both flamenco and classical music.

Guitar

The classical guitar has a wooden sound box and a neck with metal frets on the fingerboard to separate one note from the next. There are six plastic strings, stretched from pegs at the end of the neck to a fixed bridge. It has one round sound hole. The player rests the guitar on the knee and plucks the strings with the fingers of the right hand. The pitch of each string is altered by pressing – or stopping – the strings with the left hand.

Classical guitars are used as solo instruments, or to accompany singing.

The *acoustic* guitar, common in folk and pop music, uses steel strings. The *12-string* guitar is an acoustic with double strings, giving an effect of two guitars. Both are played with a plastic plectrum, or pick.

First guitar

The guitar was first brought to Spain by the Moors of North Africa.

Some great players

Classical:
Andres Segovia
John Williams

Jazz (acoustic):
Django Reinhardt

23

A great deal of craftsmanship goes into building the magnificent grand piano.

Keyboards

Harpsichords date back to the fifteenth century. Shaped like a small grand piano, they consisted of strings of different lengths stretched across a horizontal wooden frame. The keys activated little plectrums, or quills, which plucked the strings. Harpsichords could play only at one volume, no matter how hard the note was hit. Some instruments had two manuals – or keyboards – one soft and one loud.

When the **pianoforte** (Italian for 'soft-loud') was invented in the eighteenth century, hammers were used to hit the strings. The player could control the volume by playing loudly or softly by touch. This made pianofortes far more popular. They became known as pianos for short.

Grand or upright

Pianos come in two shapes. The grand piano is horizontal, like a long curved tabletop. This is because the strings are stretched horizontally. Grand pianos make a better sound than the more common 'upright' piano, where the strings are stretched vertically.

In a modern piano the low strings are thick, long, and loud, and the high strings are thin, short, and soft. So that the low strings do not drown out the higher ones, the high notes have three strings each. They are close enough for the hammer to hit all three, making the sound three times as loud. The middle range has two strings to each note, making these notes twice as loud.

Pianos are both string and percussion instruments. They can be played solo, or accompanied by an orchestra.

The **virginals** is a small, box-shaped harpsichord that can be placed on a table. A **clavichord** has rounded metal 'tangents' instead of quills, which gently brush the strings. It is so soft it can only be heard in a small room.

Some great pianists

Classical:
Vladimir Ashkenazy
Daniel Barenboim
Alfred Brendel
Murray Perhaia
Artur Rubinstein

Jazz:
Count Basie
Duke Ellington
Oscar Peterson
Fats Waller

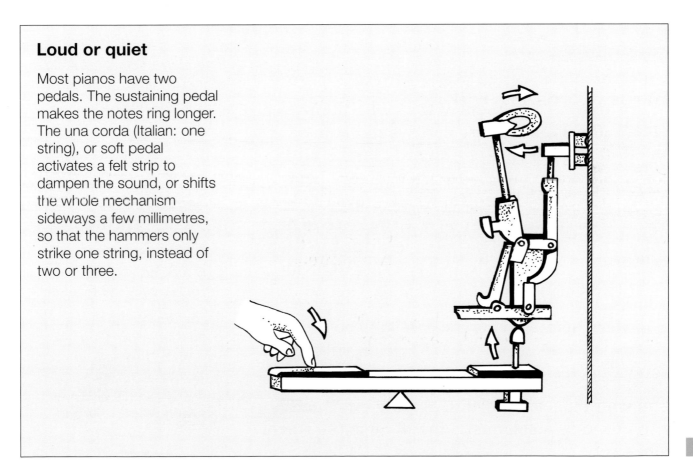

Loud or quiet

Most pianos have two pedals. The sustaining pedal makes the notes ring longer. The una corda (Italian: one string), or soft pedal activates a felt strip to dampen the sound, or shifts the whole mechanism sideways a few millimetres, so that the hammers only strike one string, instead of two or three.

The violin family

The violin family consists of violin, viola, cello, and double bass.

There are four members of the violin family. The **violin** plays the highest notes, and is the smallest. Next comes the slightly larger **viola**, which plays the middle range. Both are held under the chin. The **cello**, which plays the low notes, is played sitting down with the cello held between the knees. The extra low **double bass** is also played vertically, but is so big that the player sits on a tall stool or stands.

A modern symphony orchestra has two groups of violins, and one group each of violas, cellos, and double basses.

The violin has a beautiful, singing tone, and is often used as a solo instrument. So is the warm-toned cello.

On the fiddle!

Violins are often used in folk music, where they are called fiddles.

The double bass is used, played pizzicato, in jazz, dance, and rock bands, but nowadays its place has largely been taken by the bass guitar.

Violins are made of a curved soundbox with two S-shaped soundholes. There are four strings made of catgut, steel, or plastic stretched over a bridge. The fingerboard on the neck has no frets, so the player must judge exactly where to place the fingers to stop the strings.

Early violins

The violin is descended from viols and other similar instruments. In the sixteenth century Andrea Amati began by making violins in Italy. They made such a lovely sound that viols went out of fashion. Good violins improve as they get older. Some made by Antonio Stradivari are now 300 years old and are very rare and valuable. They are the best in the world because of the varnish he used, but the secret recipe is now lost.

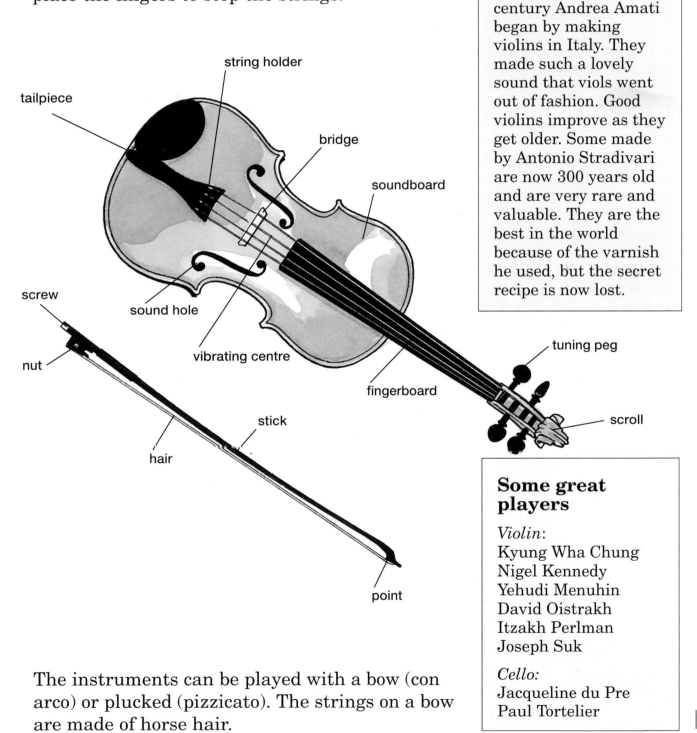

The instruments can be played with a bow (con arco) or plucked (pizzicato). The strings on a bow are made of horse hair.

Some great players

Violin:
Kyung Wha Chung
Nigel Kennedy
Yehudi Menuhin
David Oistrakh
Itzakh Perlman
Joseph Suk

Cello:
Jacqueline du Pre
Paul Tortelier

Some string instruments from around the world

Among the guitar's cousins are, left to right, the Japanese koto, the Russian balalaika, and the Indian sitar.

The **sitar** has a small, bowl-shaped soundbox, a wide neck, and up to seven strings. There are also twelve 'sympathetic' strings, which drone in the background when the other strings are being played. The strings are raised high over the fingerboard, so the player can 'bend' notes by pressing the strings down further. The sitar is only used in Indian music.

In Eastern Europe **zithers** and **cymbaloms** are used in folk and gipsy bands. They are rectangular sound boxes with strings stretched across. The zither is plucked with the fingers, and the cymbalom is struck with little hammers.

The Japanese **koto** is a large zither, shaped like a dragon's back. It has thirteen strings, each stretched over its own bridge. Each string is tuned by moving its bridge.

The **ukelele** of the South Pacific is a small, four-stringed guitar with a mellow tone. The American **banjo**, used in jazz, has up to nine strings and a drumskin sound box. This gives it its jangly tone.

Some instruments use double strings, set close together, to make a richer sound. The oldest of these is the **lute**, which came to Europe from North Africa. It has five double strings, a wide neck, a bent back pegboard, and a sound box shaped like half an egg. In the sixteenth and seventeenth centuries singers sang with lutes rather than guitars.

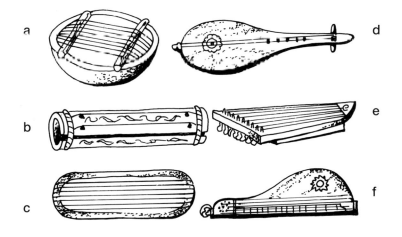

a and c, African trough zithers
b, Malagasy tube zither
d, Bornean zither
e, Finnish kantele
f, Swedish hummel

Balalaikas

Russian **balalaikas** have three double strings and a triangle-shaped sound box. The double strings are played with a plectrum played 'tremolo' – wobbled backwards and forwards very quickly. This gives an effect of lots of cascading notes.

Short and long

Italian **mandolins** have four double strings and a short neck. Greek **bouzoukis** have three double strings and a long, thin neck. Both are similar to the lute.

A great sitar player

Ravi Shankar

29

Harp

The harp dates back at least 3,000 years. The almost triangular iron frame has strings of different lengths stretched across it. The longer the string, the lower the note – but the strings must be tuned, or tightened, to the correct note. They are fixed at one end, and wound round tuning pegs at the other. The harp is played resting on the ground, and the strings are plucked.

Modern harps have pedals. They activate a mechanism for altering the key, that is, changing the pitch of all the strings at once. Many harps have seven pedals, with two positions for each pedal. Therefore very complicated key changes can be made in one foot movement.

Harps are often used as solo instruments, and their beautiful, liquid sound is also heard in symphony orchestras.

The harp produces a liquid 'angelic' tone.

Folk harps

Smaller folk harps are used in Irish, Welsh, and South American folk music.

Some great players:

Ossian Ellis
Nicanor Zabaleta

How do percussion instruments work?

'Percussion' means hitting.

Hitting a bottle produces a more musical sound than hitting a bag of sand, because a bottle resonates, or has a tone to it. Percussion instruments are always made of things that resonate, such as hollow wood, metal, or even glass.

They are divided into two groups. Those that can play tunes, like glockenspiels, are called tuned percussion. Those that cannot, like drums, are used either to keep the beat, or for special effects. They are called untuned percussion.

Some are played with the hand, like tambourines; or with fingers, like castanets. Usually some form of stick or beater is used. Others, like the piano, use keys to hit the strings by remote control. Some drums are played with a pedal.

Some percussion instruments, like the piano, which have strings, also belong to the string family.

A great player

Evelyn Glennie

The drummer is the driving force behind a rock or jazz band.

Drum kit

Drums give the beat in jazz, dance, and rock bands. The drummer uses both hands and feet.

The *bass* drum rests on the ground and is played with the foot pedal. The *snare* drum is mounted on a stand. It has a wire mesh, or snare, stretched across the skin to make a sharper sound. The snare is raised or lowered by a lever.

There are four different-sized *tom-toms*. The smallest one gives a high-pitched thud, and is attached to the bass drum. The biggest stands on legs and makes a deep, resonant sound.

There are at least two *cymbals*, plus the *hi-hat*. This is a pair of cymbals on a stand which hit each other when operated by a foot pedal.

Sticks and brushes

The snare drum, tom-toms, and cymbals are played with drum sticks or, for a softer effect, with wire brushes.

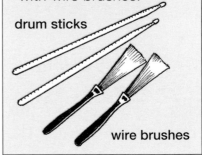

drum sticks

wire brushes

Some great players

Rock:
Ginger Baker
Keith Moon

Jazz:
Gene Krupa
Max Roach

Gamelan gongs and drums

Indonesian Gamelan orchestras are made up of tuned and untuned percussion instruments. In some ways they are like school percussion bands, but the Gamelan sound is richer and deeper.

Among the instruments are types of xylophones, marimbas, glockenspiels, and tuned gongs. The gongs look like rows of upside-down cups and bowls mounted on low stands. They are played with hammers.

All the instruments play something different. When there are up to thirty players the music becomes very complicated, but strangely weird and beautiful to listen to.

There are various drums, including a cylindrical double-ended drum which rests across the player's knees. The drums are played either with the hand or with beaters.

5-note scale

All Gamelan instruments are tuned to the Indonesian 5-note scale, which makes them sound strangely out of tune. European instruments are tuned to 12 notes, so Gamelan and European music cannot mix.

The Indonesian Gamelan orchestra contains a great variety of gongs, drums and bells.

Timpani are often called kettle drums because of their container-like shape.

Orchestral untuned percussion

An orchestra's back row can be a formidable army of hitters.

The **timpani** or **kettle-drums** are cauldron-shaped drums whose skin is tightened to play different notes. There are usually only three in an orchestra, so they do not play tunes, but their bangs must be in tune. The player tunes them during the concert.

The **side-drum** or **snare drum** has a wire frame stretched across the skin to make it rattle when played. It is used for drum-rolls and marches. The big bass drum makes a deep boom. The **gong** and the bigger and much lower **tamtam** make a deep bell-like sound.

Chinese blocks

Cymbals, large brass plates with handles, are struck together to make a crash. The tiny metal triangle makes a penetrating ping when struck with a metal rod. Wooden Chinese blocks make a clacking sound. The rattle is used for special noisy effects.

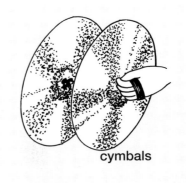

cymbals

Steel drums

In Trinidad poor but very musical people have always made ingenious musical instruments out of rubbish!

Steel drums are made from old oil drums – sometimes even from dustbin lids. The circular ends of the drums are beaten into variously sized panels, each one producing a different note when struck with a hammer. The bigger the panel, the lower the sound. The drums are mounted on stands.

Steel bands are divided into five groups. The two highest, 'ping-pong' and 'double-second', play the tunes, while 'guitar' and 'cello' play the chords. The lowest notes are played by the 'bass'.

Each note is played 'tremolo' (struck several times quickly with both hands) to give the effect of a long shimmering note.

Steel bands

Steel bands, now heard all over the world, play mostly Caribbean music, but can also play arrangements of any other kind of music.

Steel drums are built from recycled oil drums and dustbins.

Tuned percussion

Glockenspiels are made of metal strips, or keys, laid out on a wooden frame. Each key is cut to the right length to play a certain note. The longer the strip, the lower the note. The keys rest on tiny pieces of rubber, so that they will resonate when struck with a beater.

The **vibraphone** is a large glockenspiel with resonators – metal tubes sealed at the bottom – under the keys. Little fans, driven by an electric motor, bounce the sound into the resonators to make a 'wobbly' tinkling sound. It is used in jazz.

The **celesta**, used for fairy-like effects in an orchestra, is a small piano, with hammers that tap metal strips.

The **xylophone** is a glockenspiel with wooden keys, and the **marimba** is a xylophone with resonators.

Tubular bells

Tubular bells are metal pipes, cut to different lengths. They are hung from a frame and struck with hammers.

Some great vibraphonists

Lionel Hampton
Milt Jackson

Glockenspiels are found in almost every school, as they are easy to play.

Some percussion instruments from around the world

Maracas, or **shakers**, are hollow balls containing dried peas.

Gourds are large maracas with beads on the outside.

Reso-resos, or **scrapers**, have grooves scraped with a stick.

Claves are two pieces of wood struck together.

Bongoes are pairs of hand drums held between the knees.

Congas are tall, barrel-shaped hand drums perched on stands.

Timbales are pairs of drums on a stand, usually with a cowbell attached. They are played with sticks.

Castanets, used in Flamenco dancing, are wooden shells fixed to the fingers. Gipsy tambourines are hand drums with jingles.

South American music is famous for its percussion instruments. Most are found on school percussion trolleys, including the maracas from South America and tambourines from Spain, shown here.

India

Indian **tablas** are small drums played with the fingers and the palms of the hand. The **dolak** is a large, double-ended drum worn round the neck and played with clubs or hands.

37

How do electronic instruments work?

We have seen how brass, woodwind, string, and percussion instruments make sound in ordinary, everyday ways, such as blowing, scraping, plucking, or hitting. These are called **acoustic** instruments. After the discovery of electricity, electronic instruments were invented.

Electronic sound is made in two ways. The first way is to use a microphone which amplifies an acoustic sound. The second way does not use microphones, but actually creates electronic signals inside the instrument.

You can hear many electronic signals by twiddling the dial on your radio, especially on AM wavebands. The bleeps, squeaks, and long tones that you will hear are electronic interference just as traffic noise is acoustic interference.

Electronic signals are turned into sound by an amplifier whose job is to turn them into musical sounds. These sounds come out of speakers. These instruments are called synthesisers or electronic organ, and are usually played on a keyboard.

Some acoustic instruments use electricity for pumping or working a mechanism. In olden times church organs had to be pumped by an assistant. Nowadays old church organs have electric pumps. That does not necessarily make them electronic instruments, but today many modern church organs are electronic.

The microphone, not the size of the voice or instrument, is what decides the volume.

The electronic drum is more compact than its acoustic counterpart.

Drum synthesisers

Drum synthesisers play electronic imitations of percussion instruments. They are divided into two types.

The first is the *electronic drum kit*. This is a panel on a stand, covered in rubber pads. Each pad is programmed to play a different drum. Hitting a pad with a drum stick causes two wires to connect and make the sound. An electronic drum kit will have the same set of drums as an acoustic drum kit (see page 32) as well as several special effects. It is easier to carry than an acoustic kit.

The second is the *computer-programmed drum beat*. Most keyboard synthesisers (see page 40) have a set of drum beats built in. The player presses a button and the beat goes on until it is switched off. A tempo control enables the player to alter the speed of the beat.

The beat

Drum machines enable you to programme your own drum beat.

Electronic keyboards

Today's **electronic keyboard synthesisers** are cheap and popular with everyone because they imitate all instruments, and make many new sounds. Most have built-in computers which can be programmed to play accompaniments. The many gadgets make them very easy to play.

Some can even record any number of tracks – that is, separate tunes – one on top of the other. They can also be used with computers to compose and copy music – a saving on time, effort, and manuscript paper.

First keyboard
The first keyboard synthesiser was the **ondes martenot** (pronounced ornd martin-oh), invented by Frenchman Maurice Martenot in 1928.

Keyboard synthesizers not only imitate almost every instrument in the world, but also produce new sounds.

Synthesisers developed from **electronic organs** which were first widely used in rock bands. Some early organs sounded thin and wheezy, but many, like cinema organs, had a sound of their own and many special effects. Some churches replaced their enormous old organs with more modern instruments.

As pianos were too quiet for loud electronic rock bands, lighter, more portable **electric pianos** were also invented.

The **mellotron** looks like an organ, but has a taped collection of notes recorded by orchestral instruments. Using these, a player can 'magic' a real symphony orchestra, not an electronic imitation. As mellotrons are really a kind of tape recorder, with start and stop buttons, only slow music can be played. Mellotrons cannot keep up with fast fingerwork. They have now been replaced by synthesisers, even though the sounds are electronic imitations.

Too expensive

The idea of an electronic keyboard instrument was perfected in the USA by Robert Moog in the 1960s. The expensive Moog synthesisers were only used in rock bands.

Some great players

Classical realisations:
Wendy Carlos
Tomita

Rock:
Jean Michel Jarre
Patrick Moraz
Vangelis
Rick Wakeman

Using your feet

Hammond organs have a pedal board for playing bass notes with the feet. They have a special space-age sound, caused by a spinning fan in the speaker which 'throws' the sound about.

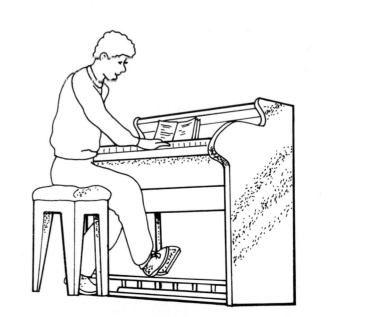

Most rock bands feature electric and bass guitars.

Electric guitars

Electric guitars are used in rock and jazz bands. They are played with a plectrum.

In the early days, tiny microphones called pick-ups were fitted under the strings of an acoustic guitar. These picked up the string's twang, or vibration, and turned it into an electrical signal. This ran along a wire and was fed into an amplifier, which turned it back into a bigger sound. This came out of a speaker.

Modern electric guitars work in the same way. They have solid sound-boxes and cannot be heard unless plugged in. They can have three sets of different-sounding pick-ups with separate volume controls.

Bass guitars have four low strings.

Steel guitars

Steel guitars used in Hawaiian, and Country and Western, music are played resting on a table. The player slides a metal rod instead of fingers along the strings, so the notes glide smoothly from one to another.

Some great players

Electric guitars:
Eric Clapton
Jimi Hendrix

Bass guitar:
Jack Bruce

Suggested listening

Benjamin Britten: *A Young Person's Guide to the Orchestra*

Antonio Vivaldi: *The Four Seasons* (strings)

Paul Tripp and George Kleinsinger: *Tubby the Tuba* and *Tubby at the Circus*

Sergei Prokofiev: *Peter and the Wolf*

Camille Saint-Saens: *Carnival of the Animals*

Maurice Ravel: *Bolero*

George Gershwin: *Rhapsody in Blue*

Paul Dukas: *The Sorcerer's Apprentice*

Charles Gounod: *Petite Symphonie Concertante for Wind Instruments*

Peter Tchaikovsky: *Nutcracker Suite*

Michael Haydn (attrib.Leopold Mozart): *Toy Symphony*

Johann Sebastian Bach: the six *Brandenburg Concertos*

Wolfgang Amadeus Mozart: *Sinfonia Concertante in E flat for oboe, clarinet, bassoon, horn, and orchestra*

Hcitor Villa Lobos: *Bacchianas Brasileiras No 2 (The Little Train of Caipira)*

Jean Michel Jarre: *Equinox* (synthesisers)

Glossary

acoustic instrument: one which produces its sound without the aid of electricity.

alto: see soprano.

amplifier: an electric or electronic device which increases the sound of a musical note.

baritone: see soprano.

bass: see soprano.

bell: the widened end of a brass instrument, from which the air escapes.

brass: a brass instrument's sound is made by spitting air down the mouthpiece of a tube. A wide opening at the other end of the tube amplifies the sound.

chord: two or more notes that fit together to make harmony.

classical music: so-called 'serious' music, rather than pop, rock, etc.

electronic instrument: one which cannot produce sound without the aid of electricity.

family: a group of instruments which are very similar, such as the violin family which includes the viola, cello, and double bass.

folk music: traditional music handed down from generation to generation by ordinary people.

keyboard: a row, or bank, of keys or buttons on a musical instrument. Each key, when pushed, produces its own sound.

orchestra: any large group of musicians formed to present music.

percussion: a percussion instrument's sound is produced by striking it to make it vibrate.

solo instrument: an instrument played on its own.

soprano: the member of a family of instruments – or the human voice – which has the highest range. The other ranges are – in descending order – alto, tenor, baritone, and bass.

strings: the sound of stringed instruments is made by scraping, plucking, or tapping taut strings of wire, catgut, or similar material.

synthesiser: an instrument which converts electronic signals into musical sounds.

tenor: see soprano.

valve: a device which can temporarily stop the passage of air through a section of a brass instrument.

woodwind: a woodwind instrument's sound is made by blowing through a mouthpiece to make a reed vibrate or by blowing across the top of a mouth hole.